POWERFUL MEDICINE

LOST SIGHT

TRUE SURVIVAL STORIES

SANDRA MARKLE

LERNER PUBLISHING COMPANY . MINNEAPOLIS

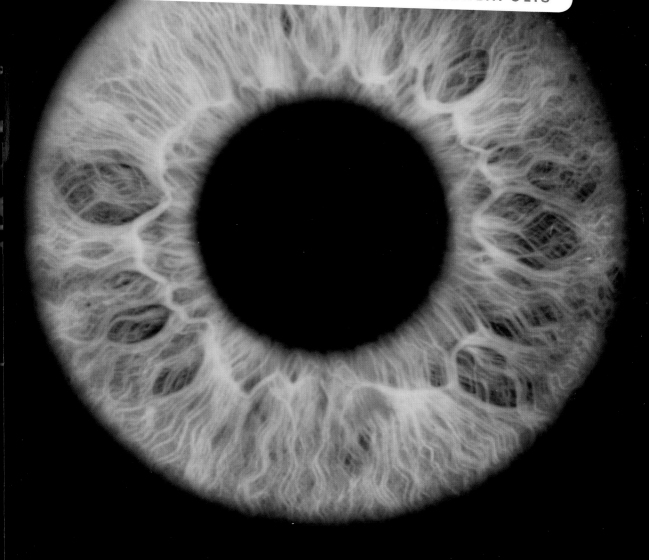

NOTE FROM THE AUTHOR

The books in the Powerful Medicine series are the result of exciting detective work that let me talk to amazing, caring physicians, surgeons, and researchers. I also got to know patients who faced challenging, life-changing experiences with determination and courage. I consider all the people you'll meet in the Powerful Medicine series heroes—their stories remarkable. Those you'll meet in *Lost Sight* are also pioneers. When I interviewed Terry Byland for this book, he said of his experimental artificial retina, "I feel like it's been huge for me to be a part of this thing. One day, as they develop even larger electrode arrays, I know they're going to help someone see in a very significant way."

Clearly, the human spirit, as well as the human body, is amazing!

FOR CURIOUS KIDS EVERYWHERE—THEY'RE THE FUTURE!

ACKNOWLEDGMENTS: The author would like to thank the following people for taking the time to share their expertise: Dr. Robin Ali, London Institute of Ophthalmology; Terry Byland; Dr. Claes Dohlman, Harvard Medical School; James Elleyby; Dr. Ione Fine, University of Washington; Dr. Daniel Goodman, University of California, San Francisco School of Medicine; Dr. Kate Keller, Casey Eye Institute; Dr. Marc Lustig, Pediatric Ophthalmic Consultants, New York; Michael May, Sendero Group; and Dr. Matthew McMahon, Second Sight. A special thank you to Skip Jeffery for his loving support during the creative process

Copyright © 2011 by Sandra Markle

All rights reserved. International copyright secured. No part of this book may be reproduced, stored in a retrieval system, or transmitted in any form or by any means—electronic, mechanical, photocopying, recording, or otherwise—without the prior permission of Lerner Publishing Group, Inc., except for the inclusion of brief quotations in an acknowledged review.

Lerner Publishing Company
A division of Lerner Publishing Group, Inc.
241 First Avenue North
Minneapolis, MN 55401 U.S.A.

Website address: www.lernerbooks.com

Library of Congress Cataloging-in-Publication Data

Markle, Sandra.
    Second sight: true survival stories / by Sandra Markle.
        p. cm. — (Powerful medicine)
    Includes bibliographical references and index.
    ISBN 978-0-8225-8701-9 (lib. bdg. : alk. paper)
    1. Vision—Juvenile literature. 2. Eye—Juvenile literature. 3. Eye—Physiology—Juvenile literature.
    4. Blindness—Juvenile literature. I. Title.
QP475.7.M37 2011
617.7—dc22   2009034443

Manufactured in the United States of America
1 - DP - 7/15/10

CONTENTS

EVANSTON PUBLIC LIBRARY
1703 ORRINGTON AVENUE
EVANSTON, ILLINOIS 60201

We go through life without thinking about how our bodies work to keep us healthy and active. Then something happens, and we realize the importance of the part that isn't working properly or is damaged by an accident. **This book will focus on a special part of our body—our eyes.** You'll read dramatic, real-life stories of people who have become blind and recovered their sight. The stories also tell of the efforts of doctors and medical researchers to restore vision. And they show how science and technology are helping make it possible for people to see again.

BOY BLINDED BY EXPLOSION

IN THE LATE 1950s, WHEN MIKE MAY WAS JUST THREE YEARS OLD, HE HAD A TERRIBLE ACCIDENT. Mike's father worked for a mining company. He had a miner's helmet with a small oil lamp on it. One day, Mike was playing with the helmet and tried to light the lamp. Suddenly, the lamp exploded directly in his face. Mike's parents rushed him to the hospital. Although he recovered from the burns, his left eye was so badly damaged that it had to be replaced with an artificial eye. On his right eye, the cornea, the clear window at the front of the eye, was badly scarred. **The accident left Mike blind.**

LIMBUS
A thin ring of stem cells—cells able to produce more cells—between the cornea and the sclera

CILIARY MUSCLES
Tiny muscles that hold the lens in place. They tighten or relax to change the shape of the lens.

AQUEOUS HUMOR
The clear fluid between the cornea and the lens. It carries nutrients and oxygen to the cornea and carries away waste.

OPTIC NERVE
The millions of nerve cells that send signals from the retina's light-sensitive cells to the brain

CORNEA
The clear part of the eye's covering that lets light enter the eye

VITREOUS HUMOR
A gelatin-like mass that fills the eyeball and helps it keep its shape. It also helps focus the light passing through it onto the retina.

PUPIL
The opening in the center of the iris that lets light reach the lens

IRIS
The colored part of the eye behind the cornea and in front of the lens. It controls the amount of light passing through the lens.

RETINA
A multilayered tissue packed with light-sensitive cells at the back of the eye. These cells react to the light. The cells produce electrical signals that are sent to the brain through the optic nerve.

SCLERA
The white of the eye. It is a tough, protective outer coating that covers all the eye except the cornea.

CONJUNCTIVA
The thin, protective membrane that covers the sclera and lines the inside of the eyelids

LENS
The clear structure inside the eye that focuses the light on the retina

Mike's parents didn't give up on their son's sight. They took him to an eye specialist. At four, Mike had a cornea transplant. In this operation, Mike's scarred cornea was replaced with a donor's cornea. A donor cornea is one that has been donated by someone who has died.

Afterwards, Mike was able to see clearly. But this only lasted for a couple of months. His body's immune system (organs, tissues, and cells working together to protect the body) attacked the donor cornea tissue. Once attacked, the donor cornea became cloudy. Mike was only able to tell bright daylight from dark.

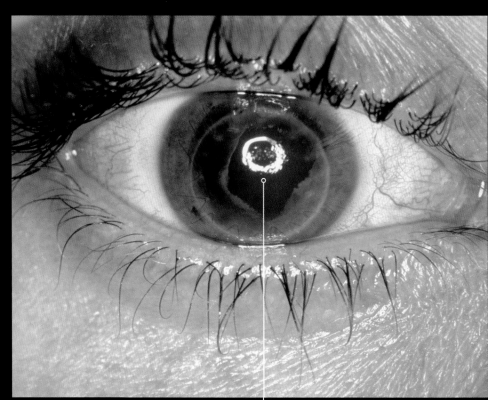

After the transplant, the cornea became cloudy.

AFTER A TRANSPLANT, LIKE MIKE'S CORNEA TRANSPLANT, THE BODY'S IMMUNE SYSTEM GOES INTO ACTION. Then special white blood cells, called T-cells, attack the donor organ or tissue. That happens because the transplant is not made up of the person's own body cells. Like other people who received transplants, Mike was given special drugs to reduce his immune system's attack response. If the drugs had worked, he would have needed to take them for the rest of his life. However, they didn't work. The drugs were not able to stop his immune system from damaging his transplanted cornea.

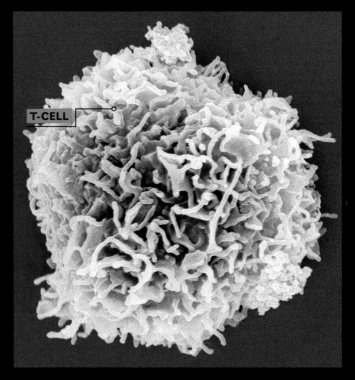

T-CELL

Mike set the downhill blind speed skiing record at the time—65 miles (105 kilometers) per hour.

A few years later, in the early 1960s, Mike received a second cornea transplant. His body's immune system attacked that cornea too. At the time, experts didn't know anything else to try that might restore Mike's vision. His parents continued to hope. They also helped their son adapt to living without sight. Mike learned to play touch football and soccer. He also learned how to snow ski. In 1984 he competed in alpine skiing at the Winter Paralympics. He won bronze medals in three events.

Mike earned a master's degree in international affairs and worked for the Central Intelligence Agency (CIA). Later, he started his own business. He was totally independent and successful without sight. Mike said, "Then I heard about a new treatment for restoring sight—one that might work for me. It wasn't [as if] I yearned to see, but it did make me wonder, 'What if I could?'"

Mike uses BrailleNote, a device he helped develop, to find places on his own.

EVERY DAY, DIRT, WIND, AND THE MOVEMENT OF OUR EYELIDS CAUSE SOME CELLS ON THE CORNEA TO DIE. This is a natural process. The dead cells are blinked away or washed away by tears. To stay healthy and clear, the cells on the surface of the cornea need to be replaced all the time. These new cells are formed by special cells, called stem cells, in the limbus. The limbus is a thin ring of cells between the eye's clear cornea and white sclera. Corneal stem cells continually produce new replacement cells for the cornea. In Mike's eyes, the limbus had also been damaged by the blast that scarred his cornea. His doctor, Dr. Daniel Goodman, thought the loss of these stem cells might be the reason his body rejected the earlier corneal transplants.

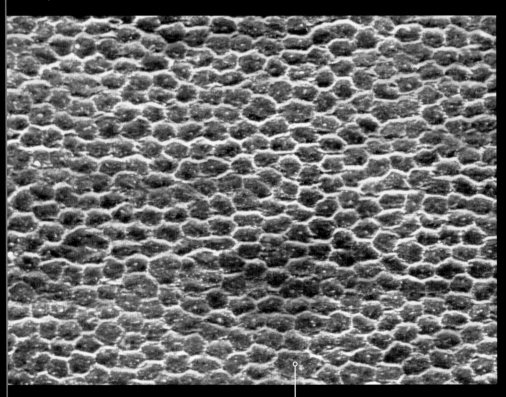

The cornea lacks blood vessels because they could block vision.

SEEING
BREAKTHROUGH

IN THE LATE 1980s, EYE SPECIALISTS FOUND A WAY TO TRANSPLANT CORNEAL STEM CELLS. In November 1999, Dr. Goodman transplanted a doughnut-shaped slice of donor corneal stem cells onto the surface of Mike's right eye. Mike had to wait about three months for the transplant to heal. **Then, early in 2000, Dr. Goodman transplanted a healthy, clear cornea onto Mike's right eye.**

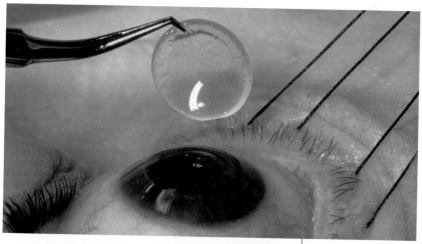

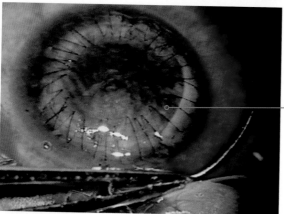

The donor cornea is cut to be a perfect replacement fit.

The donor cornea is sutured (stitched) into place.

The eye was covered with a bandage. Once again, Mike had to wait for his eye to heal. Finally, on March 7, 2000, the bandage was removed. After being blind for over forty years, Mike was able to see his wife and his sons for the very first time.

Mike said, "It was pretty special to be able to see and do things sight lets you do, like play catch with my son. What really fascinated me about seeing, though, was the every day stuff. People talk about sunsets all the time and do a pretty good job of describing them. No one ever told me there were patterns on some carpets."

Mike's right eye was working well, and his cornea was clear. But he still couldn't see details, such as faces, clearly. Dr. Ione Fine explained, "What's going on with Mike isn't a problem with his eye. It's that the part of his brain responsible for sight never learned to process visual information." Dr. Fine studied how Mike's brain functioned while he looked at things. She used functional magnetic resonance imaging (fMRI). This system let researchers see what part of Mike's brain was working and how hard it was working.

An fMRI produces images by sending short bursts of radio waves into the body. These waves make the water in the body give off tiny radio signals. A computer analyzes the signals to create an image. When a part of the brain is active, more blood flows to that part. This makes the radio signals from that area stronger. Look at the fMRI image of the brain of someone who has had normal vision *(facing page, top)* their whole life. Compare it to Mike's brain activity while looking at the same objects. His brain shows less activity. The activity is also scattered. It's not focused on the vision areas of the brain.

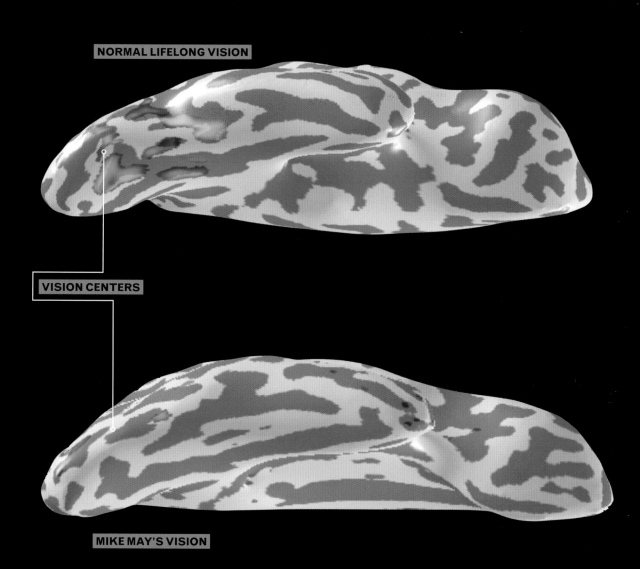

NORMAL LIFELONG VISION

VISION CENTERS

MIKE MAY'S VISION

WE SEE WHEN THE BRAIN ANALYZES THE SIGNALS IT RECEIVES FROM OUR EYES.
Light traveling into the eye strikes the light-sensitive cells of the retina, the rods,
and cones. When light hits these cells, they give off electrical signals. Then those
signals travel along the optic nerve to the brain. The vision centers of the brain are
the two lobes at the back. There the signals from the eye are analyzed and we *see*.

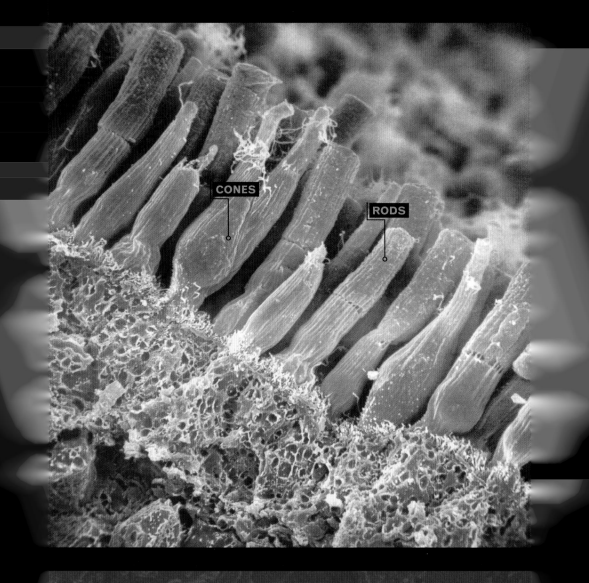

CONES

RODS

IF THERE IS A PROBLEM WITH THE EYES, THE BRAIN MAY RECEIVE FAULTY SIGNALS OR NO SIGNALS AT ALL. That can happen too if there's a problem with the nerves that carry the signals from the eyes to the brain. Anything that affects the signals the brain receives affects what it has to work with. That affects the quality of sight—or even whether the person sees at all.

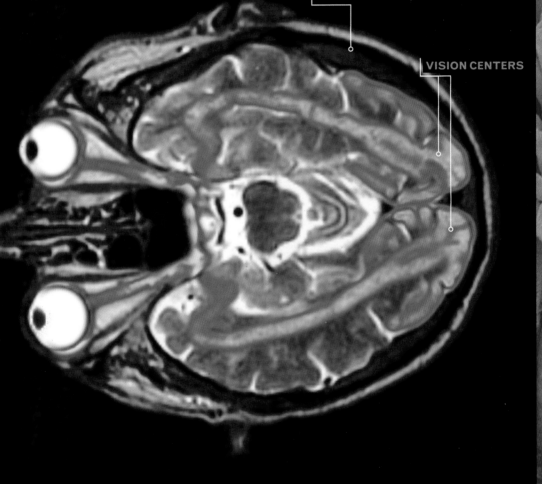

This is a color enhanced magnetic resonance image of the eyes and brain. It shows the pathways signal travel from the eyes to the part of the brain that analyzes them.

VISION CENTERS

HOPE FOR LOST SIGHT

IT WAS JAMES ELLEYBY'S OWN IMMUNE SYSTEM THAT CAUSED HIM TO GO BLIND. When he was just seven, he had an extreme allergic reaction to a medicine he was taking. The reaction caused his immune system to attack his body's mucous membranes. These are the tissues containing groups of cells that make mucous to keep parts moist. **The attack included the membranes covering his eyes. This caused his corneas to become opaque, meaning light couldn't pass through.** Like Mike, while he was still a child, James had a cornea transplant to try to fix the problem. Even though he took special drugs, his immune system still attacked the transplanted cornea tissue. **James grew up without being able to see much more than light from dark.**

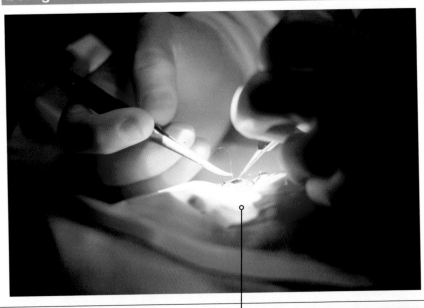

Cornea transplant surgery

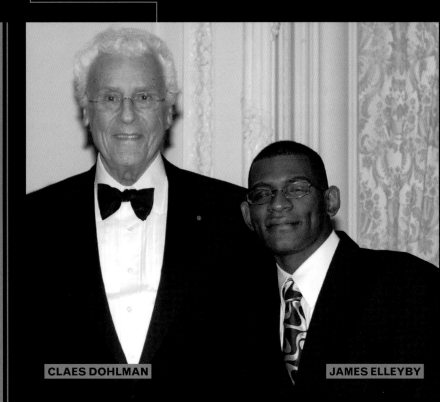

CLAES DOHLMAN

JAMES ELLEYBY

James said, "I kept thinking, 'There's got to be some
way I can see.' So I regularly used my computer's talking
software and searched on the Internet." When he was
in his early twenties, James finally found what he was
hoping for. He read that researchers had developed an
artificial cornea. Then he found Dr. Claes Dohlman, who
was willing to insert the artificial cornea into one of his
eyes. That surgery would change James's life.

The artificial cornea is called the Boston K-Pro. Dr. Dohlman said, "The Boston K-Pro worked for James, and works fo[r] other people whose bodies reject donor human tissue. That's because it's not made of human tissue. It's made of the same acrylic material used in some contact lenses."

The Boston K-Pro artificial cornea (left) *is as small as a shirt bu[tton]*

The Boston K-Pro has a clear plastic frontpiece that's held in place with a snap-on metal backplate.

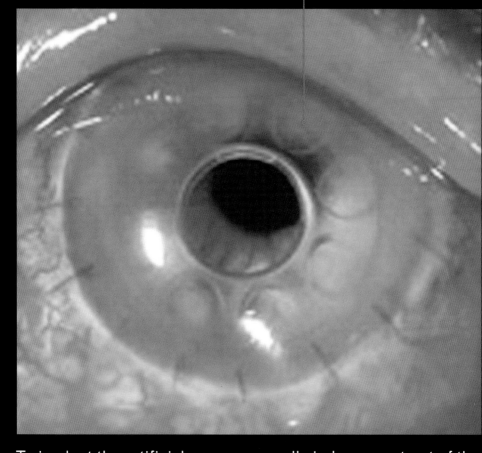

A soft contact lens is worn over the artificial cornea to protect it.

To implant the artificial cornea, a small circle was cut out of the center of James's cornea. The artificial cornea was snapped into place. Its backplate is full of holes so the fluid inside the eye can flow through it to the remaining corneal cells.The cells receive the oxygen and nutrients they need from the fluid.

James had the artificial cornea implanted in only his right eye, just in case there were any problems. He said, "Dr. Dohlman took the bandage off the day after the surgery. The first thing I saw was lots of colors. They were everywhere! They were really beautiful only I didn't know what to call them. I had to go to a class to learn the names of colors, numbers, and how to read street signs.

"Even more amazing was what I saw that first night. I remember looking up at the sky and saying to my neighbor, 'What's that up there?' He told me I was looking at stars. Wow! I couldn't believe how cool they looked. [As far as I could remember] I'd never ever seen a star before."

Even if the cornea is clear, light can be blocked from reaching the retina's cells by an opaque lens. This condition, called a cataract, often develops as people get older. Sometimes a child is born with cataracts in one or both eyes.

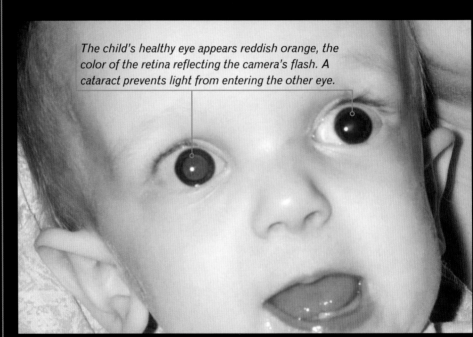

The child's healthy eye appears reddish orange, the color of the retina reflecting the camera's flash. A cataract prevents light from entering the other eye.

Dr. Marc Lustig said, "Early identification and treatment of cataracts [in children] is critical. During the first year of life, a baby's brain is [forming] its lifetime pathways for sight. If you don't restore sight quickly, those pathways are never [formed], and, even if the cataract is removed later, the brain will never be able to make sense of the signals coming from the eye."

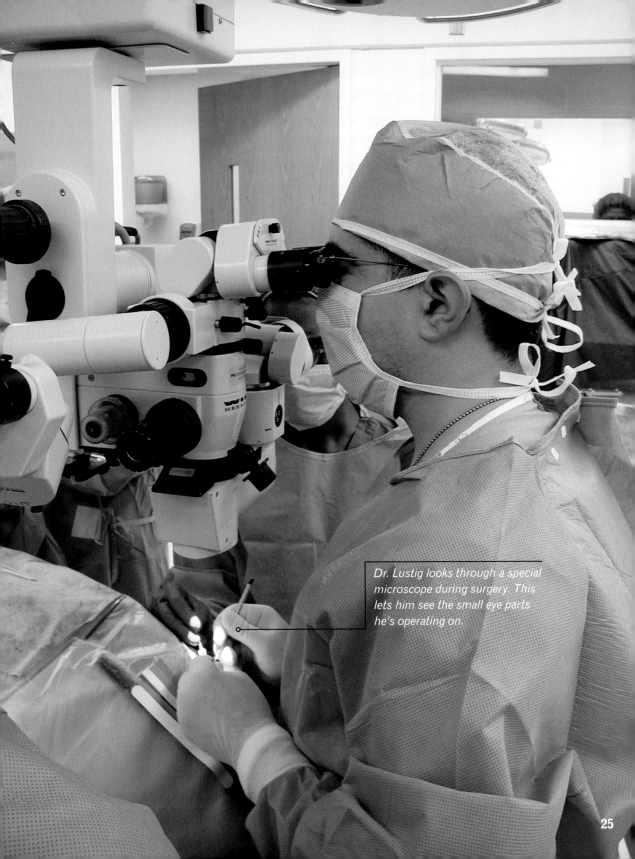

Dr. Lustig looks through a special microscope during surgery. This lets him see the small eye parts he's operating on.

To restore vision, the surgeon removes the opaque lens. The eye is able to see without a lens, but the vision is very farsighted. This means it is sharp at a distance and blurry close-up. A contact lens can correct the vision. But especially for children, an acrylic lens inserted into the eye is easier for them to live with.

Dr. Lustig said, "The only downside is that a child's natural lens is able to change shape easily, making it able to quickly change from focusing on something far away to looking at something close-up. The artificial lens can't change shape. So the child will need to wear glasses to read."

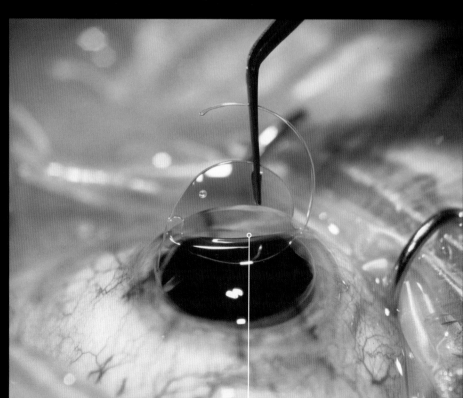

The artificial lens is acrylic,
a kind of plastic.

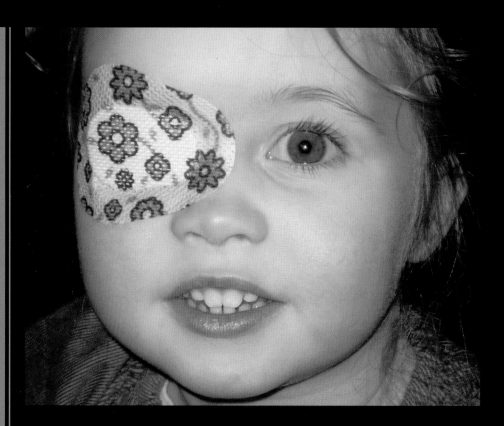

If a child needs a cataract operation on only one eye, the brain needs to be retrained for two-eyed sight. The child has to cover the normal eye with a patch for about five hours a day for at least a year. That forces the brain to make vision pathways for the repaired eye.

TECHNO-VISION

EVEN IF THE CORNEA AND LENS ARE CLEAR AND THE OPTIC NERVE IS HEALTHY, a person may still lose his or her eyesight. That can happen when a problem develops with the retina's light-sensitive cells, the rods, and the cones. The average eye has about 130 million rods, and about 7 million cones. Rods help to see in dim light and detect motion in side vision. Cones make it possible to see colors. **One inherited disease, retinitis pigmentosa (RP), causes the eye's light-sensitive cells to stop working.**

Terry Byland said, "In 1985, when I was thirty-seven, I started having trouble seeing at night. It was a year before it got bad enough for me to go to a specialist. That's when I was told I had retinitis pigmentosa and that it was likely I would lose my sight. Just five years later, I could only see what was straight out in front of my eye [as though] I was looking through a tube. Then one day I couldn't even see clearly enough in front of me to write anymore."

NORMAL VISION

RETINITIS PIGMENTOSA VISION

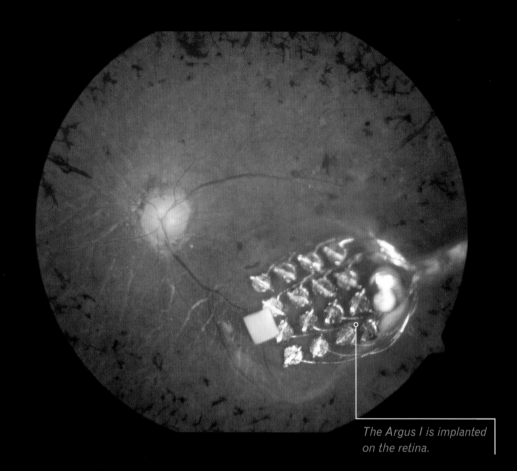

The Argus I is implanted on the retina.

Losing his eyesight was a huge life-changing experience for Terry. But with the support of his wife and children, he slowly adjusted. Then, in 2004, he heard about a new device, an artificial retina called the Argus I. Terry immediately signed up to help test it. Dr. Matthew McMahon, one of the medical team for this device, explained. "Although the [light-sensitive cells] stop working in patients with retinitis pigmentosa, the optic nerve cells continue to function. We just need a way to talk to those optic nerve cells the way the [light-sensitive cells] normally would."

To do that job, the Argus I uses a cluster of sixteen tiny electrodes implanted on the retina. An electrode is a device that passes an electrical charge from one kind of material to another. In this case, the electrodes pass an electrical charge from wires to nerve cells.

A digital camera no bigger than a thumbnail is embedded in the nosepiece of the Argus I glasses. This camera records a video image of what's straight ahead. But it's not a detailed image. It's more like a dark shadow on a bright background.

The Visual Processing Unit (VPU), which can be carried or worn on a belt, changes the camera's images into bits— like the parts of a puzzle. Then it sends out electrical signals for each puzzle piece.

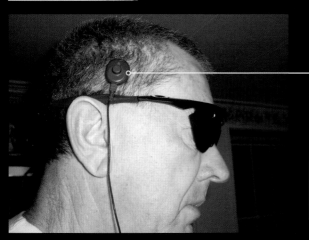

The VPU's antenna transmits the electrical signals to the cluster of electrodes implanted on the retina. Each switched-on electrode sends an electrical current to optic nerve cells. When the brain receives and analyzes these signals, the person sees the shadow shape.

Even though he could only make out hazy shapes, thanks to the Argus I, Terry was able to see his son.

Terry said, "I'm not seeing color or details. I'm just seeing dark shapes. And I can only see about 8 inches (20 centimeters) at a time so I have to move my head back and forth and up and down to look at something. That might not sound like much vision, but it is. It lets me find a doorway in a room without any help. Not long ago, it also let me see something wonderful. I have a twenty-year-old son, and one bright day, he and his friends put on dark clothes and asked me to go outside with them. While I stood on the driveway, they slowly walked in front of me. I could see them. They were only hazy shapes, but I knew one of them was my son. It was the first time I'd seen him since he was five years old. I was totally blown away."

The development team is already working on the next generation of artificial retinas, the Argus II. It will have sixty electrodes. Dr. McMahon said, "That should enable users to see even sharper images. We're also already planning ahead to develop a 250 electrode system and, one day, a 1,000 electrode [system]."

GENE THERAPY

PROFESSOR ROBIN ALI AND HIS TEAM ARE TACKLING INHERITED EYE DISEASES THAT CAUSE BLINDNESS.
They are using another approach called gene therapy. Genes are the material inside each of the body's cells that tells them what they should look like and what job they do. Inherited eye diseases are caused by genes that are either missing or not working properly. **Professor Ali has focused on a faulty gene (called RPE65) that causes children to lose their sight gradually. Steven Howarth had this faulty gene.** By the time he was seventeen, he could only see well in bright light. That was hard for him because he loved playing the guitar. He was part of a band that often played in clubs at night, but he couldn't read music in dim light. He also had trouble seeing well enough to get to and from work on his own after dark. He was eager to test Professor Ali's new treatment for his eye disease.

Steven lives for his music.

35

cells. The bacteria were left to multiply. The RPE65 genetic material increased as the number of bacteria grew. The RPE65 genetic material will be removed from the bacteria. Then it will be ready to inject into a patient.

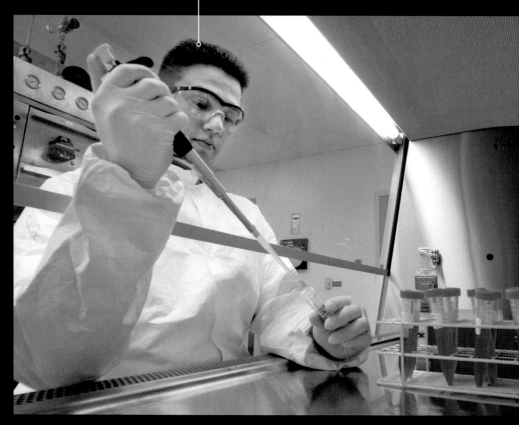

Professor Ali and his team injected healthy RPE65 genetic material into Steven's eyes. This material was placed just underneath the retina where it would affect his light-sensitive cells.

Before the gene therapy, Steven's vision was tested by having him walk around objects in a dimly lit room. It took him over a minute, and he bumped into things eight times. A few months after the treatment, Steven completed the walk without any mistakes in just fourteen seconds.

Dr. Ali said, "[Retina] eye cells never die and get replaced. So we only have to get the healthy RPE65 into the cells once to solve the problem."

The green cells in this retina hold injected healthy RPE65 genetic material.

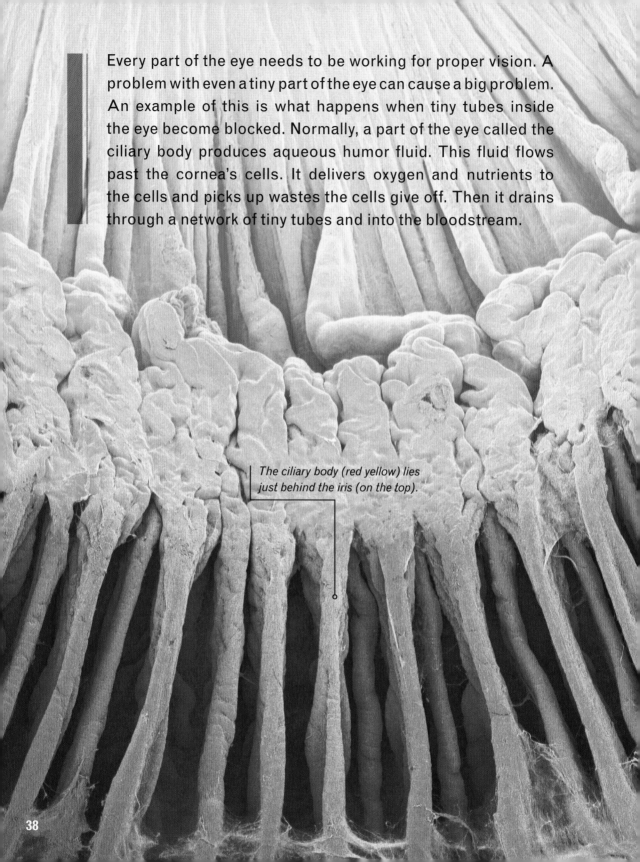

Every part of the eye needs to be working for proper vision. A problem with even a tiny part of the eye can cause a big problem. An example of this is what happens when tiny tubes inside the eye become blocked. Normally, a part of the eye called the ciliary body produces aqueous humor fluid. This fluid flows past the cornea's cells. It delivers oxygen and nutrients to the cells and picks up wastes the cells give off. Then it drains through a network of tiny tubes and into the bloodstream.

The ciliary body (red yellow) lies just behind the iris (on the top).

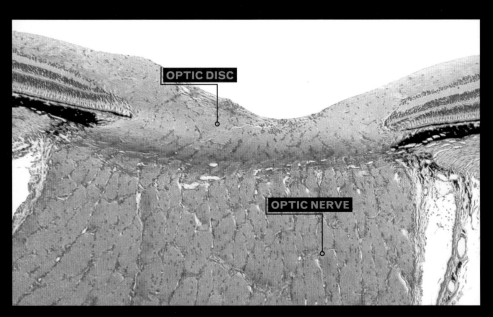

OPTIC DISC

OPTIC NERVE

Glaucoma is a number of diseases that cause the eye's network of tiny tubes to become blocked. This means the aqueous humor fluid can't drain out of the eye. As the ciliary body continues to produce more aqueous humor, the fluid builds up inside the eye. This creates pressure inside the eye—a big problem for the optic disc. The optic disc is the area at the back of the eye where threadlike nerves from the retina join the optic nerve. These nerve cells make a sharp bend at the optic disc. Increased pressure at this place can cause the nerve cells to snap. Just as broken electrical wires cut power, broken nerve cells stop signals from the eye's light-sensitive cells from reaching the brain. The greater the number of snapped nerve cells, the more vision is lost.

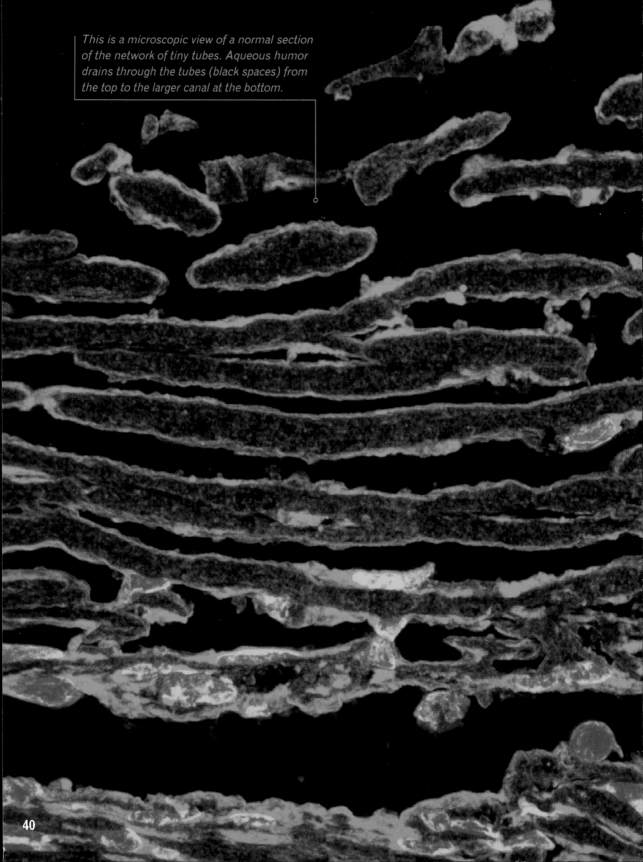

This is a microscopic view of a normal section of the network of tiny tubes. Aqueous humor drains through the tubes (black spaces) from the top to the larger canal at the bottom.

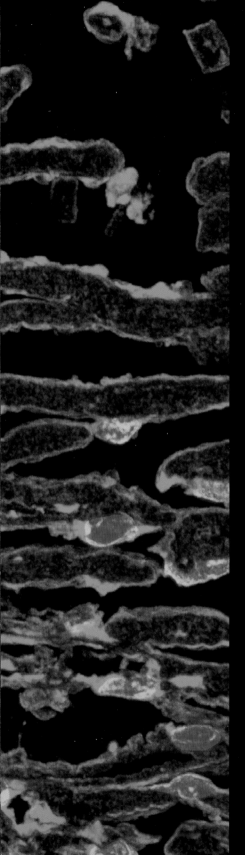

In the past, doctors knew of only two ways to open the eye's tiny tubes if they became blocked: drugs or surgery. Dr. Kate Keller is working on a new approach. She is working on stopping the tubes from becoming blocked in the first place. Dr. Keller thinks the problem is that the cells that produce aqueous humor also produce another material. This other material is what blocks the tiny tubes. She is running tests to see if injecting a special genetic material into the cells will stop them from producing the tube-blocking material. Dr. Keller said, "If successful, this genetic material would probably need to be [given every year], but compared to applying daily eyedrops or undergoing surgery, that would be a worthwhile treatment."

UPDATES

MIKE MAY continues to run his own business, which develops devices that help the blind travel independently. He also continues to ski and to enjoy time with his family.

Mike May with his family

James Elleyby (second from left)
and Dr. Claes Dohlman (right)

James Elleyby was thrilled to have the chance to share his vision success story at a recent award ceremony for Dr. Claes Dohlman. He told the audience, "Thanks to Dr. Dohlman restoring my sight, I was able to get my driver's license for the first time. I drove to this event!"

Terry Byland recently signed up for his first computer course. He said, "I'm not in the dark anymore. I have the confidence to try new things again."

Medical research, engineering, and technology are helping doctors restore sight in ways that could once only be imagined. What will happen in the future will be limited only by what people dare to dream.

Terry Byland

KEEP YOUR EYES SAFE

- Walk carefully when carrying sharp objects, such as scissors. Stay away from slingshots, bows and arrows, and firecrackers.

- Have an adult help you choose toys that are eye safe. These should have no sharp parts or parts likely to fly off and strike your eyes.

- Be careful not to spray anything, even insect repellent, close to your face and eyes.

- Wear sunglasses to protect your eyes from glare and the sun's ultraviolet (UV) light.

- Don't touch your face while playing in the dirt or with pets. After playing, wash your hands with soap and warm water. Roundworm larvae and bacteria from the soil and in an animal's droppings could harm your eyes.

EYES ARE AMAZING!

- A baby's eyes are about the same size as an adult's. However, the optic nerve and the ability to see go on developing for the first two years.

- The pupil, the opening that lets light enter the eye, increases in size in dim light. It also gets larger in response to strong emotions, such as fear.

- The average person blinks about twelve times a minute. Each blink lasts just 0.3 seconds—too fast to interrupt vision. Blinking is important. During a blink, the eyelid passes over the eye, sweeping tears across the surface. This keeps the eye moist and flushes away debris.

aqueous humor: the clear fluid between the cornea and lens that carries nutrients and oxygen to the cornea's cells and carries away wastes. An increase in aqueous humor affects the pressure within the eye.

bacteria: tiny, single-celled living things. Some are helpful and other can cause diseases.

cataract: an eye condition when all or part of the normally clear lens becomes opaque so light can't pass through

ciliary body: the structure ringing the iris. It has muscles that help control the lens' shape. It also produces aqueous humor.

cones: light-sensitive cells in the retina that enable color vision

conjunctiva: the transparent membrane that covers the sclera and lines the inside of the eyelids

cornea: the clear front covering of the eye that lets light enter

fMRI: (functional magnetic resonance imaging) A device that can show which areas of the brain are active when a person is thinking or performing specific behaviors, such as talking, looking at something, or listening

glaucoma: a group of eye diseases that cause a loss of vision when increased pressure damages the optic nerve

immune system: organs, tissues, and cells that work together to protect the body

iris: the colored part of the eye behind the cornea and in front of the lens. It controls the amount of light passing through the lens to the retina.

lens: the clear part of the eye that changes shape to focus the light rays passing through it on the retina

limbus: a ring of stem cells between the cornea and the sclera

optic disc: the area where the optic nerve connects to the retina

optic nerve: millions of nerve cells that send signals from photoreceptors on the retina to the brain

pupil: the opening in the center of the iris that allows light to pass through the lens

retina: the layer at the back of the eye packed with light-sensitive cells (rods and cones) to detect light and send electrical signals to the brain

retinitis pigmentosa: any of a group of inherited diseases that cause the breakdown of the retina's ability to function properly and results in a loss of normal vision

rods: light-sensitive cells in the retina that enable vision in dim light

sclera: the tough white outer covering of the eye

tissue: a group of cells that have a similar structure and perform the same job for the body

vitreous humor: clear gelatin-like material between the lens and the retina that gives the eye its shape

MORE INFORMATION

Want to learn more information about eyes and the latest medical advancements for treating vision problems? Check these resources.

BOOKS

Larsen, C. S. *Crust & Spray: Gross Stuff in Your Eyes, Ears, Nose, and Throat.* Minneapolis: Millbrook Press, 2010. This book in the Gross Body series investigates the science behind "gross-out" topics pertaining to the ears, nose, throat, and eyes.

Markle, Sandra. *Outside and Inside You.* New York: Atheneum, 1991. See microscopic views of the inside of the eye. Investigate the eye's structure and how its function enables sight.

Silverstein, Alvin. *Seeing* . Minneapolis: Twenty-First Century Books, 2001. Investigate how your eyes and brain work together to let you see and distinguish colors and shapes.

WEBSITES

Annie's Unite for Sight Website
http://www.uniteforsight.org/kids/eyesafety.php
This website offers fun photos and interesting activities and shares information about the causes of common eye disorders and ways to take care of your eyes.

The Eye
http://faculty.washington.edu/chudler/bigeye.html
Find lots of activities at this site that let you explore how your eyes see. Information about eye diseases and disorders and tips for protecting your eyesight are included.

Welcome to the Braille Bug Site
http://www.afb.org/braillebug/
Play games and solve mysteries to learn what Braille is, who invented it, and how it empowers people who are visually challenged.

SELECTED BIBLIOGRAPHY

NEWSPAPERS AND JOURNALS

Science Daily. "Bone Marrow Stem Cells May Cure Eye Disease." May 13, 2007. http://www.sciencedaily.com/releases/2007/05/070510160859.htm (February 28, 2010).

———. "Laser Could Change the Face of Corneal Transplant Surgery." July 10, 2008. http://www.sciencedaily.com/releases/2008/07/080707165257.htm (February 28, 2010).

———. "New Method of Adult Stem Cell Growth Treats Cornea Disorders." July 22, 2007. http://www.sciencedaily.com/releases/2007/07/070719100222.htm (February 28, 2010).

WEBSITES

Boyle, Salynn. "Researchers Developing Polymer-Gel Cornea That Would Replace Need for Human Donors." WebMD Health News. http://www.webmd.com/eye-health/news/20080516/new-artificial-cornea-shows-promise (February 28, 2010).

Laurin Publishing. "Artificial Cornea Is in Sight." *Photonics.com.* September 20, 2006. http://www.photonics.com/content/news/2006/September/20/84453.aspx (September 2008).

Neal, Rome. "43 Years Blind, Man Regains Sight" CBS News, September 3, 2003. http://www.cbsnews.com/stories/2003/09/03/earlyshow/living/main571462.shtml (February 28, 2010).

University of California, San Diego. "UCSD Study on How Newly Sighted Blind People Learn to See Provides Clues to Development of Visual System." UCSD. August 24, 2003. http://ucsdnews.ucsd.edu/newsrel/soc/sightregained.htm (February 28, 2010).

TELEPHONE INTERVIEWS

Ali, Robin, M.D., September 16, 2008.

Byland, Terry, September 20, 2008.

Dohlman, Claes, M.D., September 5, 2008.

Elleyby, James, September 11, 2008.

Fine, Ione, M.D., September 16, 2008.

Goodman, Daniel, M.D., September 7, 2008.

Keller, Kate, M.D., September 16, 2008.

Lustig, Marc, M.D., September 26, 2008.

May, Michael, September 4, 2008.

McMahon, Matthew, M.D., September 19, 2008.

INDEX

PHOTO CREDITS

Some of the images in this book simulate events that happened and are not actual photographs of the events taken at the time they occurred.
The images in this book are used with the permission of: © Paradis Media/UpperCut Images/Getty Images, p. 1; © Steve Gschmeissner/Science Photo Library/Getty Images, backgrounds on pp. 3, 5, 7, 10, 16, 17, 44, 45, 46, 47, 48; © Bruce Brown, p. 4; © Laura Westlund/Independent Picture Service, p. 5; © SPL/Photo Researchers, Inc., p. 6; © Steve Gschmeissner/Photo Researchers, Inc., pp. 7, 39; Courtesy of Mike May, p. 8; AP Photo/Marcio Jose Sanchez, p. 9; Prof. P.M. Motta/Univ. "La Sapienza", Rome/Photo Researchers, Inc., p. 10; Phototake via AP Images, p. 11 (top); AP Photo/University of Mississippi Medical Center, p. 11 (bottom); © Florence Low, pp. 12, 13; © Dr. Alex Wade, Reprinted by permission from Macmillan Publishers Ltd: Nature Neuroscience 6, 9 915-916 (24th August 2003) Figures 1 and 2, copyright 2003, p. 15 (both); © Omikron/Photo Researchers, Inc., p. 16; © James Cavallini/Photo Researchers, Inc., p. 17; © Michelle Del Guercio/Photo Researchers, Inc., p. 18; Courtesy of Dr. Claes Dohlman, pp. 19, 20, 21, 43 (top); © Robert Llewellyn/CORBIS, pp. 22–23; Courtesy of www.pedseye.com, p. 24; Courtesy of NYU Surgery, p. 25; © Antonia Reeve/Photo Researchers, Inc., p. 26; Courtesy of Pediatric Opthalmic Consultants, NY, p. 27; © Skip Jeffery Photography, p. 29 (both); © Dr. Matthew McMahon, Second Sight Medical Products, Inc., p. 30; Courtesy of Terry Byland, pp. 31 (all), 43 (bottom); © Mehau Kulyk/Photo Researchers, Inc., pp. 32–33; AP Photo/BBC, pp. 34–35; AP Photo/Paul Sakuma, p. 36; Courtesy of Robin Ali, p. 37; © Susumu Nishinaga/Photo Researchers, Inc., p. 38; Courtesy of Dr. Kate Keller, pp. 40–41; © Alyson Aliano, p. 42.

Front cover: © M. Kulyk/Photo Researchers, Inc.
Back cover: © Steve Gschmeissner/Science Photo Library/Getty Images.